NAMASTE AT HOME:

POSITIVE THINKING AND MEDITATION DURING A FREAKIN' PANDEMIC

SOLA DAMON

Library of Congress Number: 2020911395

ISBN: 978-0-578-71259-8 (paperback)

ISBN: 978-0-71260-4 (electronic)

Cover design by Alan Barnett

Cover illustration by Haley Lamborn

First print edition 2020.

www.SolaDamon.com

PROLOGUE

SANTI, SANTI, SANTI.

— BE AT PEACE, BE AT PEACE, BE AT PEACE.

*I*t's funny how different things look in the rearview mirror.

During the two years preceding the coronavirus outbreak, I had four novels in various stages of completion, traveled extensively throughout Europe and the Caribbean, and litigated large complex cases while owning and managing a national law firm. Some called it ambition. Secretly, I called it a mental illness. I suffered every moment of it.

Beneath those enviable sounding waters, with the travel and the success, I was sailing through a cesspool of personal and professional garbage. It felt as if I were in the trash compactor scene from the first *Star Wars* movie. Just as I emerged from the filthy water and caught my breath, the walls started closing in with the pandemic. It was bad. Worse than I was admitting to anyone. I've decided to keep the details vague until I'm ready to write *that* book. But to say I found yoga and meditation during those dark days would be inaccurate. They found me.

When the COVID-19 pandemic hit the US, it felt as if the scales had not only tipped, but they'd hit the floor and smashed into a million pieces. At first, I didn't make the direct association between trigger and behavior, but my accidental inner yogi desired a lot more time on her overpriced yoga mat when I, like many, feared for my 401(k), worried about my finances, and watched my opportunities deplete.

I was in the midst of coping with an (adult) child with cancer, the loss of a companion I loved, and a volatile career that had bled me personally and professionally, all with an atrociously negative and destructive mental attitude. I craved what everybody else craved: Calm. Comfort. Health. Stability.

On the Wednesday before those of us residing in California were sent into quasi-quarantine, I fell into a particular moment of anxiety that I'll gently describe as one from which I was unsure I would ever emerge. I'm not the chanty-type, but I lit a candle, sat on my yoga mat, and repeated the words from a yoga instructor named Renee Chenette. She ended every class with:

"*Santi, santi, santi.* Keep yoga in your life— on and off the mat."

Santi. Santi. Santi. (Peace. Peace. Peace.)

Each time I said the word, it sounded as if someone else was speaking. I became an observer of my own emotions, able to calm myself as if a good friend were there with me. I'd like to say the whole event was some prodigious hallowed calling, but that would be a lie. There were tears and snot involved. And on the short list of things I really dislike in life, tears and snot are near the top. Next to paper cuts. And narcissists.

So, while on that overpriced yoga mat in a cheap pair of leggings (because even a shattered girl loves a sale), this sad, former Catholic, type A, workaholic, aging, hyper-responsible, introverted, Taurus female committed herself to a martial law-like practice of positive thinking. Things had to change inside my brain to cope with what the world was throwing at me, at us, when I was already feeling down and nearly out.

My plan was simple. For twenty-seven days, I chose one card from a homemade deck of fifty-two randomly selected Sanskrit words that I crafted with index cards and a black marker. Each morning, I took five deep breaths, selected a card, researched the definition, and meditated. Then, I meditated again later in the day and practiced the process of positive thinking using the meaning and relevance of the word I'd selected. I also did thirty minutes of yoga to check in with my body. This all happened, like a devotional, for twenty-seven days in relative isolation.

Why twenty-seven? I believe in signs. Granted, maybe they're significant to me only because I believe in them. Fair enough. But even the most cynical of my friends can attest to the way the number twenty-seven appears continually throughout my life.

The most recent example happened two months before the quarantine. My neighbor, Danielle Taylor, treated me to a ticket to see Oprah Winfrey on the kick-off of her Vision2020 tour. As we waited to park the car at the venue, we talked about the significance of signs and I told her about my "number twenty-seven" history.

When Oprah took the stage, we were both astounded when, of all the random numbers in the world Oprah could have chosen to tell a particular story, she chose my number. If anyone thinks I've made up this lifelong phenomenon with the number twenty-seven, they'd have to believe that Oprah is in on it too.

I must add that any offenses taken from this book by anyone as to their beliefs, religious or not, are unintended. However, any offenses I've inflicted upon myself during this process are absolutely intentional and for your enjoyment.

Also, I am not a linguist, a historian, or a translator of Sanskrit, nor am I a therapist, although I have been called "counselor" for a long time. I'm sure there are errors in my definitions and interpretations. It takes years to understand Sanskrit and the history and meaning of the language. I apologize for any inaccuracies and embrace them as part of my soul's education. We all have to start somewhere.

At the time this book was published, the effects of COVID-19 were far from over, and so much worse than I'd contemplated in the first twenty-seven days. Editing the book was an exercise in realizing how much worse things had gotten in a short period. It went from anxieties that manifested into things like distance-shaming, weird bat stories, and the hoarding of toilet paper, masks and hand sanitizer, to hundreds dying in a day in a single state, and tens of thousands of new cases reported each day. It's still frightening.

Furthermore, it took some time after the twenty-seven day mark to get this manuscript edited, cover designed, and published. During that period, our country experienced a national tragedy when George Floyd was killed. I did not reflect on events following that atrocity in this book because the twenty-seven days I've written about preceded the event. Obviously, this book could have never adequately addressed the long overdue national conversation and reactions that Mr. Floyd's horrific death sparked.

Finally, I thank you the reader for joining me on the plunge I've taken (with no life preserver) into more positive waters. The briny cove of our inner thoughts, fearful or positive, is where the oysters thrive, hiding the pearls of who we are and what we will become. Keep swimming.

Santi, santi, santi.
Be at peace, be at peace, be at peace.

CONTENTS

KOŚA

DAY 1

On Day One, I wrote what I thought would be the first paragraph of this book. By the afternoon when I re-read it I thought to myself: "Yeah, right. What's the Sanskrit word for bullsh*t?"

But I committed, so here's what the paragraph said:

Positive outcomes await us all. When we embrace positive thinking, our limiting ideas disappear. Positive thoughts create a bridge over our negative perceptions that block the road between where we are and where we want to go.

You see? Day One of my new positive thinking practice and I'd already pulled the BS card on myself. Funny, I didn't think to make a BS card for my homemade deck. I didn't think I'd start out so frilly and Pollyannaish.

The problem with trying to be a positive thinker is that it sounds great on paper, but coming up with positive thoughts and then putting them into real practice, is terrifying. It's like walking towards a cliff and believing there are steps down to safety that you won't see until you're right on the edge.

To be a positive thinker, you have to scrounge up the

strength to believe that the next step forward really is your next step and not your last, even as you're going over the edge. We must believe in the journey even when we feel lost and hopeless.

Thankfully, the first card I drew on Day One made me laugh at myself on this daunting new path I'd committed to walking. But it also taught me to take the process in layers, like cake. I'm good at cake.

Kośa was my first card.

Pronounced "kosha," it reminded me of when I moved to New Jersey for four years and lived amongst a sizable Jewish population for the first time. I quickly learned about the practice of keeping kosher as many of my new friends and classmates (I attended law school at Rutgers) were Jewish. But with their New Jersey/New York accents, the word kosher sounded like they were saying "kosha."

Twenty-two years later, I still savor the warm memories of delis, diners, halvah, kugel, latkes, my life-long Jersey friends, being blessed with an invitation for dinner during Chanukah, and the beauty of a well-placed Yiddish word.

Kośa in Sanskrit means "layer" or "sheath." We each have five different layers, according to the Vedanta teachings (a school of Indian philosophy). The layers go from the outer physical body (e.g., skin and bones), inward to our breath, then to our mental body (intellectual), then to our spiritual/conscious layer, and then to our bliss (ooh la la.)

As an attorney who acts like David in a world of Goliaths, and as a mature (i.e., beyond middle aged) female, I must say, I rank the enjoyment of my kośas in the opposite order than I've listed them here. Bliss. I just want bliss. Is that too much for a girl to ask?

There is no bliss in the practice of law, in my opinion. Lawyers tend to assault each other, a lot. And attacks don't always come from the opposite side. By mid-afternoon on Day One, I felt like I needed five layers of thick skin to survive the shrapnel wounds after my day blew up into a massive controversy.

I wanted to be a lawyer to fight for the little guy, the underprivileged, the injured, and I've got enough piss and vinegar in me to be good at it. But after almost twenty years of fighting, I was roughed up.

And now it was Day One of becoming a positive thinker. It was "go" time. Time to start the engines and let the divine rubber hit the positive road. So when I meditated in the evening, I gingerly pushed my bad day aside and focused on the five layers as if they were strata of protective coatings I could manifest physically, closing myself off from the world. I took another deep breath and began my new practice. Seat belts fastened, here we go.

Perched comfortably on my meditation cushion, comfortably leaning back on some pillows, I started with my physical body and pictured myself mentally removing what felt like a battle-ax from my head. I was deliberate in picturing it come out of my brain with grey matter on it, and some of my dignity too, before tossing it aside. Like I said, it was a bad day. Physical layer? Check. "I'm sort of good at this," said my ego. Aaah. Another inhale, and a long exhale.

Moving inward, I focused on my breathing, on the breath layer. And that's where it got a little strange. I recall taking nine or ten deep cleansing breaths, feeling a tingling in my chest and hands, a sense of calm, and then nothing.

Two hours later, I woke up with the lights still on, and my contact lenses dried on my eyeballs like little plastic satellite dishes.

The meditative exercise focusing on my kośas seemed to have worked. Although I didn't make it any farther inward, when I woke up, I had no nagging anxiety, no palpitations, and no burning questions of a real or existential nature.

Did it work? I don't know, but I felt good about Day One, because although I wasn't particularly blissful, I'd have to say, everything felt more "kosha" than the day before.

HOLĪ

DAY 2

*H*olī quarantine, Batman!

Those were the first words that came to mind on Day Two when I pulled this card and meditated. On the highway of reality, leave it to *my* mind to try and take the humor exit.

But there was none.

On Day Two, all businesses deemed nonessential (including mine) were ordered to shutter, and social distancing was implemented with legal consequences. It felt surreal. On Day Two, I still hadn't yet ventured out into the new world with its new rules. But to draw the *holī* card, oh, the irony.

Holī isn't just a word. It's an event. A celebration in India. One where thousands gather tightly packed together for a day, throwing brightly colored paints all over each other.

I looked at pictures of it online in wonderment. Adults and children, and adults acting like children, all seemed as if they'd waited the entire year to smile, and then their glee erupted all at once on the same day. It seemed like happiness incarnate, but it sure didn't appear to be a quarantine-friendly activity.

Holī isn't social isolation, its social conglomeration. People and their germs all coming together in the name of good over evil, spring over winter, love over hate. A complete wanton exhibition of bliss. It looked like a colorful human version of a box of Fruity Pebbles had exploded and scattered throughout the streets of India. In other words, it looked amazing.

There it was, only Day Two of official isolation, and still I meditated that evening trying to visualize the day when this isolation would come to an end, and we would see color and life back in our community. I saw light blue hues in my mind during my morning meditation, and the sky was a similar color blue for most of the day.

But by the afternoon, my mind was gray and dull, and my joints ached from the pressure I could feel in the atmosphere before the skies opened up and released a seasonal downpour.

If there were colors in my evening meditation, they faded. When I took what I thought would be my last trip to the grocery store for some time, I saw grayness in the faces of those wandering around looking at bare shelves and into empty freezers. Have you ever seen the bottom of a commercial freezer in a supermarket? I hadn't. I didn't even know freezer manufacturers bothered to paint in there.

Of course, there was no toilet paper, and pushy customers behind carts tried to get the last head of lettuce.

When I got home, I meditated again and focused on humanity. I wasn't sure what else to do. I was new at this whole devotional meditation for positivity thing. The chill in the air was symbolic of what felt like a slow fog creeping in over us, so I pictured warm endings to fog-ridden days. I imagined color again soon on the grocery shelves in the form of fruits and veggies, bright and beautiful. I'd even settle for Fruity Pebbles.

I needed to believe in festivals and happiness because, in the morning, the sobering headlines announced there were more cases of coronavirus outside of China than inside of China. The global death toll had increased at an alarming rate.

It was all getting bigger and closer. And there was nothing holī about it.

VĀSTU

DAY 3

*B*efore the official stay at home order in California, many of its inhabitants were already self-isolating, which meant they were staying off the roads. The bizarre scenes on the California highways without traffic jams were a precursor to what would later become a surrealistic canvas of empty freeways, state-wide.

On Day Three, *vāstu* was the Sanskrit word I pulled from my homemade deck. It refers to where we reside in nature—our place in it.

The silver lining behind the shuttering of businesses and the lack of commuters manifested environmentally in the form of smog reduction. The air became clearer to breathe, and the views were unobstructed by the usual low-hanging grimy air.

When I sat at my desk to write, I could see all the way to Catalina Island, which sits almost thirty-seven miles off the coast of Laguna Beach, California (as opposed to the twenty-six miles from the Los Angeles area like that famous old song says.)

The air was so clear on Day Three, that not only could I

see Catalina, I could see the details of its topography including the sandy faces of its cliffs and the green hillsides where bison have roamed since 1924. Yes, bison. No, they didn't swim. They were brought over by a production company to film a western movie, but they ran out of money and couldn't afford to bring the small herd back to the mainland. (That's a true story. Google "The Vanishing American.")

Despite the clear view, my professional life was a grimy blur. I had business associates backing out of deals for self-absorbed reasons. They were literally polluting my life with a different kind of toxicity. The kind that poor human behavior spews into our lives. When I meditated, I pushed it aside with all of my might. At least I tried. I tried to use the clear view as a metaphor.

Without the usual air pollution reflecting back on the water, the ocean's blue tint was more saturated and brilliant than I'd seen it in almost twenty years. No clouds, no smog, no people. Could an unfortunate pause in our industrial nature make a difference in our air, our water, our quality of life? If I could manage to take a time out from my polluted life, would it have the same effect, mentally?

Maybe. And probably not permanently. But the idea that the air was cleaner, the water clearer, and the views longer, felt like a timeout we would have never imposed upon ourselves. Maybe I could do the same.

I meditated on the beauty of my surroundings like a silver lining, and with white knuckles, I paused all my concerns for the future.

More troubled times were obviously on the horizon, but by taking deep breaths and internalizing vāstu – our place in nature – at least it felt like we could momentarily see the horizon more clearly, come what may.

DRIŞTI

DAY 4

*G*aze. *Drişti* means gaze. Our focus. Specifically, it's our gaze during yoga poses to keep us balanced.

Our focus in yoga isn't supposed to be harsh or detailed. It's supposed to be soft and comforting. We fixate on something to keep ourselves balanced and let it blur at the same time, like looking at one of those old 3-D posters: Now you don't see it, now you do.

The morning I selected drişti, I was lying in bed writing and wondering if I had coronavirus or a seasonal allergy. I had a nagging cough that made me hyper-aware of my body, my potential symptoms, and my ability to infect someone else.

What an odd new set of fears. It distracted my focus from everything, especially the telephonic hearing I had with a federal court that afternoon, which I had to handle from home. And toilet paper. I was always thinking about toilet paper. Only four rolls left.

I tried to meditate in bed, but I couldn't fight the waves of nausea. Was it the post-nasal drip from the allergies? Or was I in that percentage of people who contracted coronavirus and experienced gastrointestinal issues? Was I actually physically sick? Or were my mental manifestations creating excuses so I could crawl back under the covers?

I gazed to the end of my duvet, and the room fell away while still hovering in the background. I repeated my emergency positive-thinking mantra, which I came up with on the spot: "I will be alright if I believe it." I said it as if the phrase was a temporary fix, like an epinephrine pen to my anaphylactic negative shock.

But my day didn't get better. My telephonic hearing with the court felt like a well-veiled panic attack. There was a sense of discombobulation amongst us all, even the judge, as we were all mutually displaced. I was exasperated not being able to put my hands on essential documents that would have been at my fingertips in the office.

When the call ended, the negative anaphylaxis set in again, robbing my ability to breathe, and I clutched the edges of my chair. *How much longer can I worry like this? It's all falling apart.*

I squeezed back tears, and I looked out my window where I saw on the horizon of the Pacific Ocean, a large white ship making its way north. Its size was equal parts daunting and majestic.

No sooner was I distracted by the ship did my neighborhood social media app blow up with pings, announcing the crossing of the United States Navy hospital ship, the USNS Mercy. I stepped to the middle of my living room and stared at her.

The Mercy has 1000 hospital beds and was making its 125-mile sail from San Diego to Los Angeles in anticipation of the outbreak's further decimation of people's lung capacities and to relieve an anticipated health care system preparing for the worst. I stared and stared and stared.

I hadn't intended to meditate after a court hearing or

while standing in the middle of my living room, but I was fixated on the Mercy, sailing bright white on the dramatic blue water. My intention, my prayers, were for the ship and those on board. I stood up and moved into four different yoga balancing poses and never took my eyes off her. When the Mercy became the anchor of my driṣṭi, I didn't lose my balance. Not once.

Driṣṭi is our strong, balanced gaze. When we find it, when we trust it, like mercy, it will protect us.

KṚIPĀLU

DAY 5

K̥ripālu means kindness and compassion. Grace.

We saw and sensed much kṛipālu in the first days of the pandemic. There were warm regards and notes on social media offering to assist anyone in need with groceries, errands, yard work, and anything else. There were air hugs and well wishes written on signs hanging from balconies. In the early days, most were kind.

My meditation on Day Five focused on those people and their compassionate efforts. But it was awfully challenging because not everyone was kind or even civil during that first week of the quarantine. And those few bad apples were good at splattering their negativeness all over the rest of us.

Spoiler alert: I really sucked at positive thinking on Day Five.

Meditation doesn't come naturally to me. I have too many sniggering thoughts riding motorcycles through my mind peeling out and popping wheelies. They kept jumping in and reminding me that my resources were dwindling, and I was down to three rolls of toilet paper while some not-so-kṛipālu-filled people were still pirating the shelves of all paper products with which they were willing to wipe their bums.

These were the same people, presumably, who were posting political tirades on neighborhood apps like Next Door that made my blood boil.

One in particular suggested that the elderly should be the ones quarantined so the rest of us could get on with our lives, which coincided with some political opinions that some of those older adults should consider risking themselves to save the rest of the world.

Um, excuse me? I had to invoke a high level of kṛipālu when it came to commentaries from social media trolls like that.

My grandfather was a World War II veteran, and my father was a Vietnam veteran. Hadn't these "elderly" people to whom these social media idiots were referring already risked their lives saving us from Hitler? Hadn't my father and his generation already risked their lives in Vietnam taking bullets over a set of poor government decisions that sent them there? Hadn't they risked their share already? Not to mention, my father probably risked his fair share plus the shares of some who dodged the draft. That's not a moral judgment, it's just a likely statistical fact.

I get it. Everyone, including amateurs, gets a platform in these days of social media overload, and more time to utilize that media when stuck at home. Even the professionals had more time during the quarantine to squawk out their 120-character idiotic tropes. Certainly not everyone can be a Walter Cronkite or a Barbara Walters whose journalism focused on facts without lengthy personal commentary and without being paid per click to increase their followers. Still, it made focusing on grace and empathy, on kṛipālu, more difficult, which made positive thinking even more essential.

I was taught that any yoga practice should start with an intention, a way to activate your receptivity and manifest that which you desire to attract into your life. My intention that afternoon during my meditation and yoga practice was for our communities to absorb a healthy dose of compassion, of kṛipālu, to get us all through this mess. I repeated a variation on a famous statement of faith as I breathed deeply: There, but for the grace of God (the universe, gratitude, blessings, or something else), go I. Go us all, actually.

Day Five summary: May our much needed collective kṛipālu, our grace, and our kindheartedness come together and protect us.

And God help me stay positive...before I punch someone in the face.

PRĀṆA

DAY 6

Pra means to bring forth. *An* means breath. *Prāṇa* is our life's force that dwells within and around each of us. It's often interpreted as "to breathe" or "to inhale." So, it seems to me prāṇa is the way we draw life's power into us.

For the first day since I made this commitment, I couldn't bring myself to meditate. The news in the morning announced that thirteen people died in a single day in New York. They couldn't fill their lungs with a single ounce of life, not even a sip of air. I felt guilty for breathing. (Who knew that thirteen deaths would soon be considered comparatively insignificant considering how bad it was going to get? Again, everything looks strange in the rearview mirror.)

I remember thinking, were these people who died sick already? Or were they stricken down from a life of youth and vitality? It didn't matter as I sat and changed my breathing from involuntary to voluntary. I made myself think about each inhale those poor souls must have gasped for until they couldn't.

It made me think back to when I was a law student. I

worked on a case for an attorney who had an altercation with another attorney who told him not to take the case so personally. But our client died slowly, and her last words were: "Mom, I can't breathe, and I'm scared." How can the thought of that moment not be taken personally?

Twenty years later, on Day Six of the quarantine, those words still hadn't left me. Patients hospitalized and isolated during the pandemic took their last breaths without anyone at their sides other than exhausted health care workers forced to serve not just as caregivers, but as the sole companions to those in their final moments before crossing over.

Before I went to sleep, I meditated again on prāṇa. To breathe, to take in life's force from the outside, to internalize it, to feed our bodies, our spirits. Life.

I set my intention on those who were still gasping for air and sent them love, energy, hope, and imaginary ventilators as if that would help. It was a desperate meditation, and I meant it. I had a feeling of desperation and fear from evoking our client's voice in my head twenty years earlier. It was the only point of reference I had to imagine what it would be like to hear someone trying as hard as they could to breathe, to stay alive.

Prāṇa, breath, is a gift. May we appreciate each breath we take and be mindful not only of those taking their last breaths, but for those who are at their sides when it happens.

YOGA

❧

DAY 7

*A*nd on the seventh day, rest.

Day Seven had a precedent for taking it easy, so it makes some cosmic sense that *yoga* would be the word I pulled even if it wasn't a Sunday. This word would be an easy one. Or so I thought.

I assumed I'd run "yoga" through the internet, consult my desk references, reflect on my own practice, cull it all down and then describe yoga the way we all know it so well and move on. Yeah, not so much.

So here's my understanding of how yoga got started, all in one breath (read with a slight tone of humor, I'm aware of the faults in my watered down description):

At some point in history, in the far east long before the Jews came back to Jerusalem, before Jesus was even a thought, and before Muhammed went to the mountain, yoga was being practiced. It's about 5000 years old, actually. It's modernly associated with Buddha, who was really a guy named Siddhartha. But yoga had started long before he was born in the mid-500's B.C.

It's likely Siddhartha was a yoga practitioner. There are

indications he studied under yoga masters which is plausible, because he was *loaded*. So loaded that the entrances to his palaces had palaces. But, since they say money can't buy one happiness (although I think it can buy a wee bit), Siddhartha left his wealth behind and became enlightened by sitting around in the wilderness contemplating the meaning of life, for years. He constantly meditated, didn't bathe, and fasted save for some raindrops, if that.

Years later when he returned to his palaces and shared his enlightenment, a movement began. A bunch more guys did the same thing, and likely employed yoga to limber up before sitting for days, unbathed, in the same position while meditating.

That's my version of the story. The details sound sketchy, I agree, but it's not the end of it. Like a late-night infomercial, wait: there's more.

Yoga means union, and not just limited to movement and thoughts. There are eight limbs of yoga according to Patanjali. And the vedas, the teachings, are thousands of years old. There are so many types and subtypes of yoga I'd never heard of as an accidental yogi that I lost track of time reading about them. Union in yoga boils down to a basic concept: It's an alliance between the body and the mind.

That's putting it plainly, and there is no way I can give the entire history and paths of yoga the appropriate attention in a single book, much less a chapter, nor am I qualified to do so. But it's an excellent place to begin.

My unlikely attraction to yoga began when I took a class where I experienced – by watching someone else fall – the pure act of being present. I'll add to my earlier disclaimer here. I'm not a stereotypical chanty, yogi-like person. My yoga practice found me when I needed a new mental path in life. I tried several classes, mostly annoyed at my inability to stay in a pose if I could even get into it in the first place.

But on one evening in a Hatha Yoga class, I did make it into a particular pose successfully and experienced an eight-second sweet-spot where I heard humming in my head and felt nothing but radiant energy running through me. The mind-body connection. It was like a plug fitting into a socket and for the first time, electricity flowed. A warm lamp turned on and I felt like light. I became the pose.

When you find that moment, the self you thought you knew falls away, but there's no doubt who you are. It feels like home.

Once you've had this experience, even if it began as an agitating one, meaning it took a lot of sweat and frustration to get there, you crave it again. It's what sends me, an inflexible introvert, back again to group yoga classes, even if I can barely reach my toes, on a good day. It's not just the physical exercise of going through the poses, it's the mental space we find open to us in a physical yoga practice.

That first week of quarantine, the yoga community gratefully began streaming online classes. It became a form of genuine union during those early days of isolation. A place where individuals could moor themselves for a sense of stability, having made it a week into their new lives. It was a place to go and see others posting joyful greetings in the comments section when they signed on to a class. Hundreds of us out there, coming together, some never having practiced yoga before. They just needed *something*.

And we didn't even know how bad it was going to get.

ANTAR

DAY 8

*R*ising unemployment. Potential stock market crashes. Uncertain futures. Fear. Worry. What will happen?

These were the headlines in our faces day and night unless you cut yourself off from civilization, which sounded refreshing, not to mention easy since we seemed halfway there.

My friend Servet Hasan, an author who survived ovarian cancer always has a spiritual joke at the ready, like this one: A man walked up to a Buddhist temple and saw a monk sitting outside. He asked: "What is the meaning of life?" The monk sitting at the entrance simply responded, "Seek within."

Antar, or *antah*, means within, inside, internal. In other words, the way I see it, *antar* consists of all those places our fears breed. Pulling this card gave me a significant inner feeling: heartburn.

How was I going to write about this one? I guess angst germinates, for me anyway, when I think about a problem for which I have no solution. And when I feel angst, I write.

My circumstances were precarious enough at the outset

of the pandemic. Not as bad as most, but uncertain enough to where positive thinking was the only option. I didn't want to dig deep within and churn up thoughts that wouldn't serve me. So I did my morning meditation at my keyboard.

I'm a touch-typist thanks to a typing teacher in the eighth grade who used to turn off the lights as she dictated strange words to us like x-ray and hypotenuse and paranoid. I closed my eyes and felt the keys, the sacred sensation of the buttons that could channel my thoughts. I typed what I sensed from the space between my closed eyes, the elusive third eye, where, for me, everything is a reddish milky void when I meditate. My fingers typed:

> There will be light.
> There will be strength.
> There will be joy.
> There will be safety.
> There will be solace.
> There will be relief.

As wonderful as those words felt on my fingertips and in my soul, when I started my workday in the unpredictable world of being a trial lawyer and in the middle of a pandemic, I was verbally attacked and humiliated by someone I'd trusted personally and professionally for many years. I felt as if my integrity had been questioned (likely an exaggeration), and by mid-day, I'd had enough. When your career is shaky, any affront feels like a declaration of war. Your emotional reactionary platform feels like it's from Texas. Everything is bigger in Texas.

Rather than strap on my armor, I "went home early," which during a quarantine meant, I shut down my laptop and walked to the other side of the tiny cottage where I stay while in California. I unrolled my yoga mat, sat down on a cushion, and repeated the same six phrases that came to me in the morning.

> There will be light.
> There will be strength.
> There will be joy.
> There will be safety.
> There will be solace.
> There will be relief.

Then, I made a cocktail.

I sat outside on my balcony and watched the ocean as I listened to people walking with their children on bikes down the neighborhood streets dying to wear out their cooped up homeschooled kids. I knew looking within was all I could do to calm myself, even if I had to slay some mental monsters to get there. I meditated and repeated the six phrases, imposing a sense of forced trust within myself. Maybe religious people call it faith.

There was nothing I could do to solve coronavirus or its effects that day or any of my other preexisting problems. And I wasn't a unicorn, so stabbing my detractors with my head wasn't an option either.

Instead, I embraced the meaning of antar. I went deep within and repeated those phrases I'd typed from instinct over and over and over until my brain had no choice but to believe them, even if only for a moment.

MĀYĀ

DAY 9

*D*ay Nine of isolation and the news was bleaker than the day before. That was the pattern, and I wondered at what point if ever, the first thoughts of my day wouldn't feel like dread from the minute I opened my eyes.

The definition of Day Nine's word, *māyā*, is: not this. Sometimes it's translated as: an illusion.

Māyā is what we refuse to see. It's the illusions we create in our heads to avoid facts that are true whether we want to believe them or not. Sort of like death. We don't want to face it, but it will come to us all. Our refusal to embrace it, that's māyā.

Since the best way to avoid creating illusions is to accept reality, the intention I set for my morning meditation focused on acceptance. The virus was taking hold of everything. I was tired of fighting the hopelessness and avoiding the new abnormal. Acceptance of these circumstances is what I sought. So I tried to embrace the following eastern philosophy: There is neither good news nor bad news, there is only the way we react to the news. There are only facts to be accepted. But the effects of the facts surrounding COVID-19 were gaining on us.

With no normal schedule to follow, I took a walk in the middle of the day. Maybe I hadn't noticed it before, but by Day Nine people instinctively knew what six feet looked like when distancing.

My entire North Laguna Beach neighborhood was taken over by pedestrians with a new unspoken agreement that one person would walk on one side of the street, and one would walk on the other, even if headed in the same direction. When a third person entered the picture, someone automatically veered right down the middle of the street to keep the appropriate distance. Those in cars got used to navigating through the pedestrians, ignoring the white and yellow lines, allowing everyone their space. Hopefully.

Our new patterns of movement in public reminded me of my girlfriend, who worked in Washington DC when the infamous "DC Shooter" was on the loose. She described the "looney walk" commuters adopted while walking through the District. They would take a few steps then dramatically shift their direction to the other side of the sidewalk as if doing a fast-paced walking hip-hop dance. The theory was that the sharpshooter, wherever he was, wouldn't be able to keep a steady aim on a radically moving target. She said pumping gas was even weirder, like hopping up and down behind the car and between the gas pump to keep the potential crosshairs off your head.

Funny. Isn't that what we were starting to do? Avoid a viral sharpshooter from taking aim at us? Minus the looney movements, of course. Still, it was the adoption of a new set of circumstances that involved distance, masks, and acceptance of the facts. The truth.

Our bodies are built to rewire with habits for survival,

but they don't rewire automatically to accept the truth. The virus was creeping its way through our population.

There were no illusions by Day Nine. There was no vaccine, and more people in our collective communities were getting sicker. In my life, before becoming an attorney, I received a Master of Science degree in public health. I specialized in toxicology, but the public health principles were drilled into us: Epidemiology, virology, and concepts such as herd immunity. It was these truths and potential truths we were forced to face at the outset of the pandemic. Facts empower us, even while scaring us.

When I meditated in the evening, I set my intentions on the health care workers and first responders on the front lines facing the suffering. Our politics, opinions, conspiracy theories and protests were luxuries, illusions, māyā. Our health care workers on the front lines didn't get the luxury of māyā. They faced reality every day.

APĀNA

DAY 10

*I*f *Prāṇa* is the life force we inhale, *apāna* is the exhale. Inhaling indicates stress, exhaling indicates the relief of stress. It's our energy as it descends.

To exhale doesn't just feel like breathing, it feels like breathing *again*. When the astronauts landed on the moon in 1969, the NASA engineers on the ground waited in anticipation with no control over the outcome. The minute Armstrong announced the Eagle had landed, Houston responded:

"We copy you on the ground. You got a bunch of guys about to turn blue. We're breathing again."

Inhaling feels as if we've jumped off a cliff. Exhaling feels like we've survived it. Inhaling feels like a trip to the moon. Exhaling feels like landing on it.

When I pulled this card, my meditation was predictable, or so I thought. Breathing. How hard can it be? We do it without thinking about it. Inhale, exhale. Prāna, apāna. In, out. Ebb, flow. The message is the same in each direction: Be present and make the natural next move.

The most comforting part about taking up a meditation

or yoga practice is that once you make the choice to do it, the practice meets you where you are, at your most basic— your breath. It's just waiting for you to pay attention to it.

Day Ten was a Sunday. The biggest news was that the Summer Olympics might be canceled (and they were), the police might be called upon to limit the crowds trying to see the cherry blossoms in Washington DC, and eight states had issued stay-at-home orders. The latter was in sharp contrast to what would be the status of Day Twenty-Seven (and beyond) when almost every state was on lockdown of some sort, and the death toll skyrocketed.

My therapist texted to make sure I knew I could still visit with her online if needed. The text was a reminder that I might have been hiding behind my ability to be a loner, an introvert, a bookworm. It was a reminder that the best thing to do when facing uncertainty is to face it. I went back to the mat to meditate. It was becoming a new source of distraction. In a good way.

Apāna. What does it feel like at the end of an exhale? For me, it's the most comforting part of breathing. The only thing to do after an exhale is to inhale again. There's only a feeling of satisfaction to look forward to.

There's also a scientific explanation for the relief of an exhale. When I studied toxicology, we experimented with chemicals that would affect the *sympathetic* nervous system, which is at the heart of our fight or flight response. Inhaling is linked to it. We take deep, sharp breaths when we're panicky.

Exhaling is connected to the *parasympathetic* nervous system, which is our body's inner spa and wellness center. Exhaling is about relaxing, feeling a sense of relief. As humans, we forget the simplest of notions: Relief exists inside of us already. Comfort is in the exhale. The signals from our parasympathetic nervous systems are sent out when we breathe deeply and exhale thoroughly from the stomach. We can summon relief if we breathe deeply often enough because exhalation is the tonic our bodies crave when the future looks bleak. We produce this effect all on our own.

When you pair this biological reaction with the purpose of meditation and yoga, and its native language that describes it (Sanskrit), the tonic becomes even more soothing. Add mindfulness to your breathing (mindfulness being the ability to observe your thoughts without letting them carry you away to that place where emotions take over complete control), and you've got body and mind working together to produce a calmness from which you can address your reality.

On the mat for my afternoon meditation, I took a deep breath and exhaled, riding it out longer than the inhale. I did it twenty times and envisioned sending my negative thoughts away as if blowing them out through my nose to oblivion. Some forms of yoga practice use multiple rapid exhalations after a single inhalation, like the breath of fire practice in Kundalini yoga. The breathing made me tingle, made my body more tranquil, and my thoughts more clear. Maybe not more positive, but brighter, as if someone had pulled the curtains halfway open.

Day Ten ended calmer than when it started. Sometimes it's the little things that get us to the next day with some peace if we stick with the practice.

NIRVĀṆA

DAY 11

*F*or personal and professional reasons, I live in two cities on opposite coasts: Laguna Beach, California, and Fort Lauderdale, Florida. Thankfully I am considered a local in both. And I must say, calling these two places home, well, as they say, it does not suck.

I spent most of February and March 2020 in Fort Lauderdale, and had intended to stay longer. But with the outbreak of COVID, I chose to quarantine in California where my two (step)sons live, one who was undergoing chemotherapy at the time. I couldn't risk getting stuck anywhere but there, near him and his wife.

Because of my history with these two cherished cities, both dependent on tourism, I know what pain looks like for business owners when the tourists don't show up as expected. In Laguna Beach, the small businesses began to feel the full effect by Day Eleven. The town that welcomes six million visitors each year might as well have started welcoming tumbleweeds.

Nirvāṇa, like yoga, is a Sanskrit word that has taken up comfortable residence in the English language. We tend to use nirvāṇa in place of the word bliss, as if it's a feeling. But nirvāṇa, in Sanskrit, is an achievement. A place we arrive. Only through exhausting oneself with no more ability to sustain human wants and needs and by shedding earthly feelings like loss, despair, desire, or grief, will we have reached nirvāṇa, an eternal state of peace.

I was sitting in Nirvana on March 19, 2020, when the Governor issued the official "stay at home" order in California. (No, really, I was. One of my favorite local Laguna Beach restaurants is named Nirvana Grille.) It's across the street from my office and over the years has become a sanctuary some nights. More significant than that, is how Nirvana had already prepared for the reality of small business survival (even before the lockdown) while providing its community with essentials: They became a grocery co-operative.

When I pulled the nirvāṇa card on Day Eleven, I tried to think of a way to describe the path to a post-coronavirus peace. It didn't work. I couldn't even picture the idea of going back to everyday life without being slathered in hand-sanitizer and surrounded by paranoia, not to mention the illogical mask haters.

I meditated about the journey we were all on, facing circumstances we've never encountered before, some more dire than others. When I sat down to craft this chapter, I tried again to describe, to imagine, the post-quarantine nirvāṇa we would reach— the journey through the rules and the consequences, and the reward of a simple glass of wine and an appetizer in a restaurant sitting close enough to a stranger to say things like, "That looks delicious. Where was that on the menu?"

All I could think about was the decadence of that evening eleven days earlier at Nirvana Grille. It was the last night I'd eaten in a restaurant. I missed salmon chowder, chicken wontons, a smoked poblano chili with chicken and artichokes, mussels in butter with skinny fries dusted with paprika, and rosemary bread washed down with a Villa Maria sauvignon blanc. Every bite tasted like a last meal, without us knowing at the time that it sort of was.

I also thought about the owner, Lindsay, who grew up in Laguna Beach and kept that restaurant thriving even during tough times. She had turned the bar area and the bar itself into a grocery store with fresh produce and homemade dressings. She was the chef on-hand to pack your requests and give you advice on how to cook it when you got home. She and her skeleton team, all worked the front and back of the house to fill orders they received online for their gorgeous items from the menu, or pre-packaged groceries, including paper products, which was a big deal while the shelves were bare. She used her ability to source products wholesale and passed them on to the community.

My meal at Nirvana Grille was the last supper of life as we knew it. It was the last night restaurants were open for a seated meal in California. Sadly, some shuttered for good. Fortunately, Nirvana's grocery co-op still serves the community along with the delicious civilized-feeling of having gorgeous meals for takeout. (Later, it re-opened as allowed under California mandates).

I set my intention when I meditated that night on people like Lindsay in our communities (and everyone at Luigi's in Fort Lauderdale) surviving this storm. As humans, we may not reach a complete form of bliss in this lifetime, but sometimes if we work towards appreciating a piece of the present moment, we may just get a taste of nirvāṇa.

DUḤKHA

DAY 12

My girlfriend lives with a great guy. They're both considered essential workers and have been serving the community with essential services, putting them at risk of contracting COVID-19. He admitted to her that his biggest fear is that, because they are unable to quarantine and are exposed to the public, that she will contract the virus and die alone on a ventilator. Or worse, he will get it and infect her, and then she'll die alone on a ventilator.

This story simultaneously warmed and shattered my heart. His fear was real. If she got sick, he wouldn't be allowed by her side. He loves her to no end. It would kill him. Just thinking of the scenario made me so sick I had to shut it out of my brain. It's the ones left behind that hurt the most in this mess, and people suffer legitimately from "pre-fear." The fear of losing their loved ones before they become, if ever, sick with COVID-19.

It was Tuesday. Tuesdays were becoming weird for me. My Mondays were a hectic combination of that typical Monday feeling mixed with the anxiety of doing my job with fewer resources while trying to pull off a sense of status quo.

Tuesdays felt a bit more settled but spritzed with Monday's messy leftovers. Basically, Tuesdays were gloomy.

This practice of thinking positively, challenged me harder by Day Twelve because not only was it a gloomy Tuesday, the card of the day was *duḥkha*.

Duḥkha means all the things associated with the pandemic: sorrow, grief, suffering, stress. It doesn't have a singular translation. It means the unpleasantries related to the human condition. But also buried in the definitions was the idea of impermanence.

When I meditated that morning, it was harder to focus. Harder to be positive. I could feel a sense of unity, but not in a good way. I felt part of a collective where everything was getting tougher, and we all wanted to stay in bed.

I started this twenty-seven-day practice because I, like most others, felt like a window had shattered when the pandemic hit, and the wind and rain were destroying the house slowly, paint chip by paint chip, one moldy rug after another. I committed to this practice because I needed to change my attitude for survival, and that need for change was emerging mostly as a need to practice more acceptance.

Like the Serenity Prayer, I strived to accept the things I couldn't change, but I also acknowledged that such acceptance is not automatic. We're human and subject to sorrow and grief and all the other human sufferings— the duḥkha. We aren't wired to accept dire consequences and tragedy instantaneously. We aren't wired to accept them at all. More often, we try to fix them or deny they're happening.

It was only twelve days in, and it had gotten easy to lose a grip on reality, gratefully. Because the reality was, things were getting even worse.

I meditated in the afternoon with the intention of solace. I referred back to the definition of duḥkha. It included impermanence, the notion that we may suffer, but it too shall pass. Fascinating. Like solace is automatically built in to suffering.

If our negative human conditions came with instructions, the suffering section would likely say: automatic, or batteries included. But the part of the instructions that might address our ability to accept our human suffering as impermanent? That part would read: major assembly required.

It takes work to make the intensity of our emotions impermanent. We need support, hope, and a healthy dose of believing in ourselves to pull that off. Not to mention tapping into our divinity, which isn't easy. In the end, we must wrench the faith from ourselves to believe that what this pandemic is doing to us will *not* last forever. Nothing ever does.

To recognize something's impermanence feels like performing real magic. It gives us control over our emotions rather than handing that control over to the circumstances we find ourselves in.

Circumstances are never eternal. Granted, the occasional meltdown is completely appropriate when blindsided by horrible circumstances. But a slavish adherence to the belief that bad circumstances are here to stay will kill anyone's spirit. And and that kind of death is preventable.

I didn't know on that particular Tuesday, twelve days after starting this practice, if I was any more successful than anyone else at being a positive, hopeful person. But I did feel an ounce of relief each day I followed through with my commitment. There will be suffering, but there will also be light. There will be strength. There will be joy. There will be safety. There will be solace. There will be relief. I repeated the words again, as I had on Day Eight, until I believed them. Again.

KAIVALYA

❧

DAY 13

*W*ednesday. The end of March. Day Thirteen alone in my California cottage by the sea— a writer's dream. The scenario looked good…on paper.

My routine while working from home involved waking up, making coffee, shuffling the Sanskrit cards I'd made, and researching whatever word I pulled from that homemade deck. Then, I'd meditate. When I was finished, I'd shower and commute to work via the bedroom to my desk in the living room. A whole seventeen steps. Coffee in one hand, my ritualistic morning smoothie in the other. Yep. Living the dream.

But I woke up on Day Thirteen with a headache, some nasty emails, and it was about to get worse.

When I shuffled the cards, I pulled the Sanskrit word *kaivalya.* It means isolation. Solitude.

"Well, I could have told you that," I said to the pile of index cards through my squinty eyes. The pressure in my head felt as if my eyeballs would shoot from my skull and splat on the wall.

I didn't expect the imposition of positive thinking on my psyche to be an effortless process, but I thought it would be an encouraging one. It really wasn't, or so it felt that morning. I forced myself to meditate.

Sometimes I laughed at myself sitting silently and cross-legged. Sometimes, I didn't sit cross-legged at all. Sometimes I took "corpse pose" on my yoga mat and laid there like a dead person wondering how I could have lived this life differently. But no matter what, I always came back to my breath.

"It will be okay. There's no other choice," I would say out loud.

But back to the word of the day: kaivalya. The original purpose of meditation was to move towards enlightenment. To be so detached from the physical and material earth that you are one with the supreme light. Isolation with meditation is supposed to lead to the ultimate truth.

There's no doubt that kaivalya when sought and achieved voluntarily, must be a delightful experience. Complete and utter serenity must flow from the attainment of total isolation from the material world. But I wasn't feeling it. Probably because seeking enlightenment wasn't the reason we were isolated.

Day Thirteen was the first day I started to lose my nerve. My livelihood was on the line, and I was watching others lose theirs. I'm an advocate by nature and training. I couldn't help anyone return to normal. I couldn't even help myself. The variables were daunting. The future unclear. I wanted to protect the world, and in turn, myself.

Day Thirteen also brought a superficial layer to the experience. All those memes about gaining weight in quarantine were no longer a joke. By Day Thirteen, I'd put on weight, and missed visiting with the locals in my small beach town. I missed visiting with other business owners there too. I missed hovering over the produce at the grocery store without worrying about touching things and not wearing a mask. I missed squeezing and smelling fruit at the farmer's market. I missed the samples at Trader Joes. Tasting those, now *that's* a daily practice I could devote myself to, no doubt.

I thought about going to a restaurant inland to visit friends but caught myself mid-thought. *Not possible.* There was nothing to do in the form of the usual Wednesday happy hour. No prosecco and ceviche at the restaurant at the end of my street overlooking the water. (The irony of seeking opportunities to eat and drink as a reaction to complaining about weight gain was not lost on me.) I thought about planning a trip for my birthday at the end of April but stopped short of booking a flight because the latest news rumored the shutdown wouldn't be lifted by then. (It wasn't. And how funny it is that I actually thought it might be.)

I was determined to find the upside of isolation and edited four chapters of a novel I'd been writing. I cleaned the kitchen. I returned emails and long overdue phone calls, simultaneously making human connections and fulfilling obligations.

Still, isolation efforts without immediate returns on the investment turned out to be unsettling. Was I living up to all my obligations? Was this world that had come to a halt still passing me by? Every phone call made me feel as if life was moving on successfully for others, despite the pandemic, while I was still floundering.

Setting aside my anxious nerves, the day still seemed promising, at least that's the positive spin I forced on the day as part of this practice. I journaled about the gratitude I should have been practicing instead of focusing on the persistent inner clock ticking away the minutes, the days, the months I had left in me to survive through this with my finances intact.

I meditated at sunset and said "thank you" out loud ten times in a row for what I did have, and then once more, loud enough that anyone could have heard through my open windows. I had more than I'd ever thought I would have in life. I had more than most. It was the fear of losing it that I was letting control me.

I wanted to make sure that God, the Universe, the Supreme Being, Shiva, and all the deities and forces that might be out there understood how grateful I was for everything I had. But I felt nothing. So I decided the best way to be positive was to be positive for others.

With no volunteer opportunities during the shut down, I spent the rest of the evening cleaning out my closet of clothes I'd never wear again and prepared a donation to Working Wardrobes in Irvine, California. People would need jobs when this was over. They would need clothes. They would need shoes. I could provide two out of three.

When I was finished, I think I'd psyched myself into a zone I'd created via seemingly unimportant chores. Isolation is for enlightenment. Enlightenment is about gratitude. Gratitude deepens with service towards others. I could isolate if I could find ways to make it about someone else. Goodness knows there were situations worse than mine, even before the pandemic. I'm white (I was also thin and blonde most of my life. I'm very aware of the privilege that's all given me), I'm educated, and I have assets, albeit dwindling. No matter how bad it was going to get, I'd have it easier than most in the recovery period after this pandemic cleared.

Note: My service in gathering donations was not wholly selfless. I sipped a sizable dirty martini in a tumbler with six olives while doing it. Hey, they were big olives and a girl's gotta eat.

I never said I was an expert at this whole positive

thinking thing. I was thrusting it upon myself come hell or high water, and I would be the first to admit, it wasn't always pretty. It was, however, a hell of a lot more comfortable than most would experience under any circumstances.

Grateful. Grateful. Grateful.

BANDHA

DAY 14

I meditated with one eye open on Day Fourteen. Two official weeks in quasi-quarantine, and I was dying to be distracted by anything. What was that outside my window? A crow? A giant bald eagle in the middle of suburbia? A blue-footed booby bird? (It could happen.) Better go look!

The card in front of me on Day Fourteen was *bandha*, which means to lock in place. To be bound. Well, well, well. Not to mix my French with my Sanskrit, but during a quarantine, how *apropos*.

Would this ever end? Two weeks of being locked in place and even me, a devout introvert, was feeling the need for humans. Not the interactions we'd been relegated to on the phone or community apps like Next Door, where neighbors tattled on neighbors for not appropriately socially distancing. There was a feeling of cabin fever and a craving for even meaningless social interaction.

I took a deeper dive into the word and learned that bandha also means to hold, as in a pose. It's a key concept in yoga: To bend in a way that blocks the flow of energy or blood to specific areas of the body to allow a surge when released— sort of a physical or spiritual bottleneck that creates a subsequent, healthy rushing flow.

Then I got to thinking, with all of us holding in place, was the quarantine causing a societal bottleneck? A societal bandha? Would we surge back into society with renewed energy for a more rewarding and meaningful future amongst each other? Or would the blockage stop up our bad human behavior and cause us to come back with an angry or spiteful rush of reintegration?

The isolation forced upon us would likely cause us to be better or worse versions of our already existing selves once we were allowed back into society, together. Maybe we'd become a bunch of indoor feral creatures who, when released from our public health bandha back into the world, would take our hoarded toilet paper and TP our own houses.

Can you imagine it? Like a whistle being blown and suddenly we all run out there trying to live like we used to but too caught up in the excitement of no limitations? We'll probably look like kids running around with no rules, doing things like putting our mouths directly on the self-serve frozen yogurt tap, filling our mouths and loving the ice cream headaches, begging for more. "Yes! Yes! Now vanilla!!"

Can you picture shivering from the bliss of putting a bare hand on a door handle, and then turning it without the concern of what might be on it? Or the relief of not searching your car, your purse, or your pockets for a mask you need in order to walk in to most establishments?

Or what about scratching your face without a tissue and not feeling the urge to slather yourself in anti-bacterial goo? The day I can do that I will ooh and aah like it's an orgasm. God I miss scratching my face.

Hey, no reason positive thinking and this staying in place bandha thing can't be fun for a hot second.

KULA

DAY 15

*C*ommunity. *Kula* means community. Or maybe clan. As in people. Lots of them. People living upstairs from people and around the corner from people, and near people, waving at people, relying on and interacting with people.

Are you kidding me? This is the word I pulled from a sloppy homemade stack of cards I crafted into a deck after I spent the entirety of my previous days not having a single conversation with a single soul that wasn't typed in a text or on email or via FaceTime or Zoom?

It's good to know the Universe has a sense of humor, even if it did bring some virus into our lives that isolates us, kills people, and sucks our toilet paper into a black hole. Probably the same black hole to where all our single socks, pen caps, keys, and all the other things we've lost have gone.

So, what does the sense of community mean when one meditates? What can be conjured up during a pandemic? Community. Kula. There were 101,000 reported cases of coronavirus in the United States on Day Fifteen. Really not a great card to have pulled. Except that tragedy sometimes builds communities.

Later in the day, a friend sent me a link to a story about neighborhoods putting teddy bears in their windows to make kids smile. To give them something to do, like finding them on a scavenger hunt.

There was even a story about drawing pictures of colorful Easter eggs and hanging them in windows so kids could walk or drive around and have a virtual Easter egg hunt on Easter Sunday. And then the famous "clapping" videos of entire cities flickering their lights, honking their horns and clapping at the precise time the shifts changed at local hospitals. That's community. That's positive thinking.

The intention for my evening meditation was very simple: Namaste. May your health be strong, and your heart be light. From my kula to yours.

MEDASVIN

DAY 16

*J*f I were texting the definition of this word, I would have started its description with: LOL.

Medasvin. Let's just jump into a bowl of old-fashioned Jello pudding here. The nonorganic, really sugary, whole milk, artificially tapioca-flavored kind. And then let's roll around in its preservatives for a while and love it because medasvin means "fat." A more civilized way of describing it might be "corpulent."

Oy vey, my New Jersey friends would say. I thought: *Great. Just when you find yourself in the throes of hanging on by your thumbs with the only thing between you and the ground below is your ability to think positively, you gain weight too?*

Being home all day gave me access to food all day. I was confident I would come out of quarantine the size of a hippo with a gland problem.

Even shopping during the quarantine brought out altered states of food behavior. While limiting my trips to the grocery store as ordered, I tended to load up on things I could store in the freezer, things I would typically never buy. I had an overwhelming feeling, for example, that I might just need calcium someday, and if my supplements ran out, well ice cream has a bit of calcium, and it can stay frozen for long periods, right? Brilliant!

The problem wasn't so much the ice cream. It's that it was staring me in the face all day when I opened the freezer depressed, anxious, scared, tired, or indulging in a temporarily skewed self-care moment.

Ice cream in a lactose intolerant person enclosed indoors in a small home. What could go wrong? It's not like there was anyone around to see me blow up like a tick and then hear me deflate, right?

But the point was, and is, to be positive. Medasvin also means robust and strong. It's how I promised to keep my sense of humor throughout the ordeal.

So, I ate some ice cream and skipped meditation and yoga. The day got chalked up to self-care, self-indulgence, and self-reflection. The lifestyle I'd been leading never allowed me an opportunity to sit alone and inhale bad food. There was always too much going on. Coming home wasn't about enjoyment, it was about rest, recharging, and figuring out new things to worry about. The pandemic gave me the opportunity to enjoy a simple carton of ice cream and laugh at myself when I reached the bottom.

And it's a good thing, because every ounce of humor was sucked out of me the next morning. Let's just say, the news was filled with a corpulent wake-up call as to how much worse things were getting.

PARĀBHŪ

DAY 17

*T*he news reports on Day Seventeen could be summarized as the following: Refrigerated trucks were filled with bodies outside hospitals in New York to relieve the morgues. There were over 2400 deaths in the United States. (Again, if only we knew how few that was considering how bad it would be come July.)

It was March 29, 2020, and the President announced that the lockdown would continue until April 30th. Another thirty days felt like a death sentence to the economy, as it had been for the deceased. And it was Sunday again, which by Day Seventeen didn't feel different from a Tuesday or a Friday. Everything melted together in a mixture of bad news, stretchy pants, and angst.

My morning meditation with my Sanskrit cards felt like a welcomed habit. Sunday was a day I could spend more time on this process, and I realized the daily practice I'd come to rely on, in relatively short order, was a source of anchorage and gratitude. Which resulted, I noticed, in a slightly more positive attitude.

On the weekends, I'd started to keep track of when my

mind went negative and how many times I pulled myself back from it. I kept a journal. My world hadn't improved, but my attitude had shifted a bit. I took stock more often. I still had a roof over my head, a couch to sit on, a furnace that worked during an unusually rainy cold snap in the ordinarily mild Southern California weather. Grateful, grateful, grateful.

There are multiple definitions and interpretations of the word *parābhū.* I tilted my head when I read the word. I'd slept in a little and still had bedhead and blurry eyes. Back while making this deck, when I scribbled out the cards with a Sharpie, I didn't spend much time on pronunciations, I just selected words randomly.

Parābhū, sounded like "paraboo," when I said it out loud. It bounced off my tongue as fun words do. "Paraboo." Igloo. Cuckoo. Muumuu. Emu. Doo-doo.

But the definition wasn't bouncy or fun at all. Here's the sampling I culled from my print and online resources:

1) To defeat, vanquish, overcome;

2) To hurt, injure;

3) To disappear;

4) To perish, be lost;

5) To submit, yield;

6) To suffer a loss;

7) To succumb.

One would think I googled "emotions and effects of COVID-19."

Parābhū. "Pah-RAH-boo." To succumb.

It takes time, I imagine, for a body to succumb to something. For a human soul's shell to yield to that which will steal its breath from this life. The beautiful physical machine we were each given in the form of our body, will capitulate eventually to something. This virus seemed a more unnatural cause of demise to those who had succumbed. Like a thief in the night who showed up, sent to steal everything from us.

The coronavirus' force of parābhū – its ability to injure – was carving out its scars and making us look at the potential of it. The emotions of it. The psychology of losing to it. By Day Seventeen, at least 2400 people had succumbed to the potential the virus could exert over us, and hundreds of thousands were injured by it. There was power in that.

But there's also power in the human spirit to survive. Another definition of parābhū is to defeat and overcome. The ability to walk through the fire and live with the scars. The power to believe we won't vanish and disappear in the wake of physical, emotional, or financial losses. The pandemic's path was not destroying us, it was just changing the face of the inevitable. Birthdays were still celebrated, albeit from a distance. Babies were born, only not ideally with both parents present. Weddings were postponed, but the commitments were tested. The scars came in different shapes and sizes for all of us.

Three weeks before the stay-at-home order in California, for various reasons, I attended a writing conference at the Kripālu yoga center in the Berkshires. It sounds fancy, but Kripālu is an odd place for an introvert. The first interaction I had was at dinner the first night. Kripālu has cafeteria-style food service, which was delicious, but it felt like high school on the first day. Who will I sit with? Will anyone like me?

I got my tray, stood in line at the buffet stations, filled my plate, and walked the length of the cafeteria, looking for a friendly face next to an empty chair.

"Do you mind if I join you?" I asked a young woman sitting by herself.

Her sweet face completely welcomed me. Her name was Cara, which I didn't learn until after twenty minutes of conversation because when I asked her why she was attending the conference, we became engaged in stories about our kids. One of her sons had passed away, and one of my (step)sons was in chemotherapy. And although that might have defined us outside a place like Kṛipālu, inside, we were women overcoming what life had dealt us and nurturing new fragile lives we'd brought into the world: Our own, as writers.

Cara became an example of positive thinking for me. Death had already visited her, in the worst way. She felt her child's last heartbeat as he succumbed to the freak accident took him away. But she chose the positive definition of *parābhū*. She decided not to yield to the grief. She chose to overcome and survive her loss.

My intention during my evening meditation was to be more like that. Someone who chooses the positive definition, the positive outlook on a situation. Someone who, instead of choosing to submit, or disappear, chose to defeat and conquer the injuries handed to her. She honored her grief by carrying it, but she also used it as a tool, not a hindrance.

Less than a month after meeting her we were quarantined and I really began to fall apart. But I knew it then. I would be hard pressed for the rest of my life to think of a better role model for positive thinking.

OM TAT SAT

DAY 18

*T*he day I pulled this card, there had been over 570 deaths in one day in the United States due to coronavirus infections. Five hundred and seventy souls. Meditation was taking second place behind checking the news as part of my morning routine. It became impossible not to.

The rearview mirror effect: Wouldn't it be great if we could get back to those numbers? By the Fourth of July weekend, the new daily reported numbers were beyond 50,000 cases per day.

Om Tat Sat. It's not a word, but a phrase for which there are so many definitions: Thou art that. All is that. The three mantras of salvation. The absolute truth.

The difference in translations seemed to be, through my untrained eye, a result of the vast nature of the words "om" and "sat," whereas every source I reviewed pretty much agreed that "tat" means "that."

Om. This is the word we all say when we want to make fun of yoga-like stuff. It's used in sitcoms by hippies hanging on to their pasts. But om is essential, universal. It means everything. It didn't start as a word. It began as an internal sound recognized amongst early yogis when they meditated. Whereas we read it as one word, it's actually made up of four sounds in one. Au-oh-mmm, and then silence. Chanting om repeatedly is supposed to connect our physical existence with that of all things in the universe. It is called the universal sound.

Tat. Tat means that.

Sat. Sat means true. Honest. Real. That which is.

With these meanings in mind, I conjured up my interpretation under the circumstances. I decided on the following definition of om tat sat relevant to the times: Experience everything as honest and real.

When I meditated on the words, om tat sat, I let them slip from my lips. Om flows evenly and comfortably, but tat and sat have harsh tones, like a prickly form of onomatopoeia. It wasn't soothing, but neither were the headlines: Five hundred seventy deaths in one day. More to come. Global shutdown. Yet it seemed we were meant to experience it all, everything that is honest and real. Pandemics included.

I went back to om. Om is a vibration, a feeling, a calling to bring about the same vibration in others. A sense of all was the only thing that could bring balance to the rest of this crisis. It encompassed the good and the bad. It was the only way to reach the end of my rope and with no option but to be positive. All or nothing was coming. Whichever showed up, I was ready to look it in the face and smile.

Om.

ABHYĀSA

DAY 19

*P*ractice. *Abhyāsa* translates to a practice that focuses on the effort to reach a tranquil state of mind. An exercise we continuously pursue to remain balanced and in harmony.

Day Nineteen: Balance found a potential ally.

When I took notes each day to prepare for writing this book, sometimes it seemed like I was writing in a ship captain's log. I tried to keep the facts clear as to what was happening each day during the quarantine. The day before marked the milestone of 570 deaths in a single day, which made it difficult to want to do anything the next day.

Thankfully, the first reports of hopefulness came on Day Nineteen. The number of cases was still increasing, but the rate seemed, momentarily, in some areas to be, maybe, possibly, dropping. Social distancing may have taken hold. Hope may have found an opening to show its shiny little head like Punxsutawney Phil on Groundhog Day.

I meditated on this card longer than I had in previous days. Could it be?

Abhyāsa isn't just *a* practice. It's the word in Sanskrit *for* practice. I set the card on my cushions, where I meditated every morning, then took it with me over to my mat, where I fell about into different yoga poses. Practice. My practice. Showing up with intention. Showing up period, again and again, with no attachment to an outcome, only intentions.

On Day Nineteen, a friend sent me a link to a story about a man who had several bottles of hard to come by hand sanitizer and left them at his doorstep for the delivery people arriving at his home to take so they could keep themselves protected. It was a practice of kindness.

The practice of breathing deeply through stress, of staying balanced, of seeking solace in our minds to keep us healthy. The practice of being grateful to everyone working in essential positions. The practice of appreciating that delivery people continued dropping essentials at our doorsteps, and charitable organizations assisted those who lost their jobs, and all the others. The practice of merely appreciating each other as humans. The abhyāsa of gratitude. Practice. Practice. Practice.

The good news about the rate of infection dropping seemed almost too good to be true. Hope is fragile. It can disappear even if the wind only threatens to blow. No practice would guarantee a change in our collective outlook, but there was the practice of holding on to hope as individuals, and sharing it with all.

Practice positive thinking. Practice understanding. Practice kindness. Practice connecting to others. And then do it again. Practice.

PURUṢA

DAY 20

uruṣa means spirit, an individual soul, or that which remains unchanged and independent of everything. The word represents our one true self. Our core. It is not of this earth. It is not part of the physical world.

I meditated on the word puruṣa the morning of Day Twenty breathing each syllable as I inhaled and exhaled. When I was finished, I focused on the street outside. The postman still delivered the mail.

I'd never waved at my postman, probably because I was never home to see him. But I did after my morning meditation. He barely acknowledged me with one end of his mouth curved up. Maybe he didn't know how to react. Perhaps it was a sign of the times. He looked so tired.

Puruṣa. That which remains unchanged and independent of everything. It's also sometimes defined as a story, where a cosmic man sacrificed himself to the Gods to create all life. All religious and spiritual teachings involve a tale of sacrifice similar to this. And many religious teachings represent the standards by which all should live, in the form of stories and symbolism, and provide the illumination by which we should lead our lives, if we choose to believe.

This begs the question: Isn't that what essential workers like my postman and medical personnel around the world had been doing every day?

Essential workers had been sacrificing their health so that others may live and carry on with their lives from day one of this pandemic. They risked exposure from patients, from packages and letters, and each other, not knowing if their co-workers were silent carriers of the virus. The doctors, the nurses, the EMTs, the postal workers, the grocery store staff, the drug store clerks, the street sweepers, the hardware store workers, the police officers, the firefighters…

What if we were to organize our mind as if our positive thoughts were essential workers? They must remain unchanged and independent of everything else. Our positive thoughts must adapt and keep showing up, believing that we can make a difference, thinking we can surmount the troubles facing us.

I only accomplished ten minutes of yoga the evening of Day Twenty, but I meditated again right as I dropped to the mat. It felt as if the days were caving in on me. On the one hand, my professional life came to a standstill. On the other, I was getting phone calls for new work where I was expected to operate as if it were business as usual. I was walking the plank, believing there was a rescue boat down below bobbing along the whitecaps waiting to catch me when I fell off the edge.

I took deep breaths and made a commitment to myself. I promised I would attempt to have a new relationship with reality, regardless of the circumstances I was panicking over. That's what essential employees do. That's what first responders do. Adapt to the scene you find yourself in, take a deep breath, and believe you can move forward towards a positive outcome.

I meditated again and repeated these words while envisioning a hospital room full of doctors and nurses treating patients: Thank you. You are the ways and the means through which we all will survive this. Thank you.

NADĪ

DAY 21

I awoke from a dream about water, about being drawn to it. Feeling it beside me, as if it were alive, and I wasn't. The card I drew that day made sense.

Flow. *Nadī* means to flow. It can mean a river, or it can mean our blood and the vessels through which it flows. It describes the life force both in us and around us.

My morning meditation felt good on Day Twenty-One, until the phone rang. Problems at work sent me down the dark path I was eternally facing in my professional life unless I forced myself to be hopeful. I felt like a plane crashing, and a voice in my head was yelling, "pull up, pull up!" I had to walk away.

And I did. I walked and walked. I live near the ocean, and the windy weather had turned the shoreline into turbulent hammering waves crashing on the sand, before pulling back in long swaths of white foam. As torrential as it seemed, there was a rhythm to it. There was a flow. The waves came, and they went. But they always came back.

Nadī is to flow like water. To find the path of least resistance. To go with the power of nature.

My natural ego-centered power that day was filled with rage. I accepted that. I accepted that to flow I must allow myself to feel, to understand what made me angry, helpless, like a failure. This life will let us flow as long as we don't fight it, even as it drags us over the rocks, because our spirits know where our lives are traveling. We can't act like helpless lumps, but we must understand the flow. The beautiful trickle, to the babbling brook, to the raging ocean, back to the calm shore.

I felt like a failure because that day the pressure of my world combined with the circumstances of a pandemic confused all that I'd known for the past twenty years. But after watching the water, it was easier to push the day back into the flow and believe that the swells would recede. The storm would pass. To accept the flow, the nadī and its process, would lead to calmer waters, again.

BHĪTI

DAY 22

*B*hīti means fear. The thing we all were trying not to feel during the anxiety of the COVID days.

In yoga and meditation, we're taught not to get upset when a negative emotion makes an appearance in our head-space. We're supposed to act as the bouncer at the door of our swanky inner sanctuary (or nightclub) called "Self-Care." Smile at the negative thought, acknowledge it, and ever so kindly, deny its entry into your pulsing beautiful happy place.

When I made this makeshift deck, I randomly selected words without considering that some might be negative. In that sense, my deck had what we call in the legal arena a "design defect." Or maybe not.

Bhīti doesn't just mean fear. It means anxiety, fright, terror. It's a word that feels alarming. So, with this word, I started writing first instead of meditating, and it ended up setting the tone for the last five days of this twenty-seven-day process.

Emotional fears are learned behavior. We serve as our

own sources of them. Not that our fears aren't real. I read several articles about fear after pulling this card, but understanding it didn't make it go away. Fears are part monster, part security blanket. Terrifying things that provide you the cover you need so you never have to change and be uncomfortable.

So, on day Twenty-Two, I decided to accept the fear I could feel in my emotions and my environment. The government was telling us to make masks. My financial health was getting scarier. The world was taking a crushing blow that seemed to be the tip of the iceberg. And there was nothing I could do about it.

As difficult as it was, I sat down and forced myself to breathe through this one. This one card that felt like a lousy prophecy, like a wrecking ball to the steps I'd taken over the last twenty days to make myself a more optimistic, hopeful person.

I closed my eyes to meditate only once that day, and instead of using the word as the intention, I opened my mind to allow whatever thoughts chose to appear. And they did. Positive and negative. I asked the negative ones to step kindly aside. Here is what I let in:

This is not forever.

This moment will pass.

Change will serve you.

Fill your mind with warm thoughts.

Believe the journey is taking you where you need to go.

Be grateful.

Be grateful.

Find something to be grateful about. Immediately.

My eyes were closed so tight they twitched. When I opened them, everything looked the same except the sun had begun to set, and orange light poured in.

I took three more deep breaths and made dinner. I accepted the fears lingering around the house, but I didn't set a place for them at my table.

DHARMA

DAY 23

*W*hat steadies us and keeps us from falling? What is constant? What keeps us on track like the navigation app on our phones? Is it our sense of internal law? Because it seems like abiding by the rules and responsibilities we impose upon ourselves is what gives us scaffolding. Having boundaries keeps us from falling into chaos. But what happens when the scaffolding of life as we know it starts to fall away?

Those were the first thoughts that flooded my mind on Day Twenty-Three. I know because I wrote them down in the journal I keep in my bed. Then I looked at my phone for the headlines. Which famous person had the virus and died? What's the latest? Mask? No mask? What's happened to the stock market?

I didn't even get out of bed that morning. Instead of coffee first, I meditated under the covers after pulling a card.

Dharma. I'd seen this word before. An employee and dear friend gave me a card deck for Christmas called "The Wild Unknown Animal Spirit Cards," by Kim Krans. The deck is full of beautiful drawings and comes with a booklet with beautiful explanations of the spiritual nature of certain animals. Some mention dharma.

My research indicated that our dharma should be one's guide through transitional times. Dharma is one's most profound purpose. The message of dharma is: listen. Listen to what your deepest voice, your righteous voice, is telling you to do.

The COVID-19 outbreak felt like a vast social experiment of what people felt their dharma was. Some people's righteous voices didn't seem to care about the stay-at-home orders. The charming thing about our species is that we have free will. Yet, when it came to the pandemic, the overarching concern was that one person's free will could mean someone else's death.

My evening meditation, you'd think, was a wonderfully focused intention on the laws of the universe and righteousness because that's what yoga and dharma and meditation and spirituality should be about. That's not exactly how it went. It's the human part of life that always gets in the way. Take a perfect idea, and we humans will figure out a way to muck it up.

Example: On Day Twenty-Three, 630 people died in New York City. The image of 630 bodies stacked up was unbearable. What dharma, what deep spiritual purpose could be found in 630 souls leaving us on the same day because they couldn't breathe? What priest, guru, rabbi, shaman, imam, or pope, could provide a reason for that? Where was the comfort? Where was the mercy? Docked in Los Angeles and New York, not fulfilling their dharma, that's where they were.

The USNS Comfort was in New York and had a total of twenty-seven patients on it. The irony of *that* number under *these* circumstances was not lost on me. Not a good sign, this time. Doctors made controversial statements critical of the waste of resources bobbing on the water, while people lost their lives in local hospitals.

Dharma is supposed to be what holds us together. I reached down deep during this crisis like everyone else and couldn't find it. I could only see a patchwork of kindness here and there, from time to time, that served as glimmers of hope.

Like the local "safari" my neighborhood designed, where people placed stuffed animals around their homes while parents drove their kids around slowly down the streets in their hermetically sealed cars to point out all the different "big game" animals. The clapping campaigns to thank health care workers. The random "thank you" I heard spoken to public workers in the community. It's as if the world was watching others answering their duties, other people's dharma, and applauding.

I wondered, what would be our dharma in the coming weeks and months? What will hold us together? We're fighting a foreign war. It's neither of the World Wars, nor Korea, nor Vietnam, nor Iraq nor Afghanistan. It's a war that will see how we behave against each other on the same side. We're supposed to be in this together. Even if I still can't find toilet paper, hand sanitizer, or a thermometer.

Like any war, we need good leadership. We need someone to identify our cohesiveness in this, as a community, as a country. How long would we have to wait for that? Which potential leader will step up and recognize their righteous self and begin to shift this story?

My intention during my evening meditation was to focus on my own righteousness. The commitment I made was to be a positive force. Until better leadership showed up, we could only control our own behavior. I made it a point to act out the common meme on social media that says: Be the change you want to see in the world. I gave out what I wanted to see and what I wanted in return. It wasn't all yogi-like, or touchy-feely, and it took an effort to get away from my inherent doomsday attitude. But it was genuine, and it felt so much better than being miserable. I meditated with the intention that I could be the change, and the change would happen.

Baby steps, one smile at a time.

LOKA

DAY 24

Loka means "the world." The universe.

It was Sunday again. The Old Testament reports that God created the world in six days. That's a lot when you consider when He started on Monday, the earth was just a big massive void. By Friday, it had light and whales and birds and all the other creatures. He must have gotten pretty fired up about the whole project because then He made humans and thought it would be a good idea to let them run around unsupervised.

No doubt when day seven rolled around, God needed a nap. Imagine all that bureaucracy and planning. Getting the birds to stay in the air and the fish to stay in the water, and the ducks and flying fish wanting to be both places? A logistical nightmare.

Then the humans thought it would be nice to raid the garden for a snack and couldn't keep their hands off each other, which led to some labor and all sorts of kids and grandkids with weird names. I needed a nap just thinking about it all.

When I pulled the loka card, I thought I'd transition from

my version of the earth's story from the Old Testament to outlining the sh*tshow it had become with hundreds dying each day. But where would the hope be in that? What kind of positive thinking would that be?

I convinced myself to make it a Sunday where I would go out of my way to appreciate every little thing.

I went for a walk, a long one. The kind where you get lost in your surroundings. The birds, the sky, all the things we take for granted, including having healthy bodies. I looked forward to hyperventilating on pure, natural air. I wanted to get high from taking too many deep breaths. And I did.

I watched the mockingbirds and the crows, the finches, and the hooded orioles. I watched the waves roll in and chase the seagulls from their feast of sand crabs, their skinny legs a blur of speed.

We take the world, our loka, for granted and sometimes for good reason. We're busy with our lives, the ones we had before the pandemic. It's our western culture to do so, whereas, in eastern religions and cultures, humans are not at the center of the universe, they're just characters in its story.

There's a bit of relief in realizing how insignificant we are in the big picture. Like being cosmically let off the hook. The outcome of this mess would affect me, but it wouldn't be the earthquake I was preparing for— it would be a small fact in the world's history, no matter how bad the outcome might be. It would be alright. We are just creatures in a managerial role, according to the Old Testament. Merely characters in the universe's play.

And since I was just a character, I returned from my walk and did my second meditation on my balcony with a Sunday mimosa, because as a human acting in a role, I could make choices. Plus, it felt like a civilized thing to do.

As a child, I lived on an island considered a British territory. Setting aside the barbaric practice of colonization, I was exposed to things considered "civilized." Like visiting the Lawn Tennis Club where gin and tonics were served like water while hummingbirds flitted around sucking on puffy peach hibiscus flowers. I watched a hummingbird for ten minutes on my balcony, which became part of my meditation. I breathed in appreciation and gratitude. I exhaled calmness and energy.

Coincidentally, I checked the news when I came inside and saw that Her Royal Highness, Queen Elizabeth II, had just given a rare address. It was a message of hope where she likened her broadcast to the one she gave with her sister in 1940 during World War II. Both messages were meant to comfort the sense of isolation and fear that both situations, although different, were delivering. It was a message steeped in positive thinking.

And long live the Queen's message, I thought. A woman whose own elderly son contracted the virus. She was an example of the stalwart nature we'd all need to embody going forward. As the sticker says: Keep Calm and Carry Om.

I might add that when I checked the news and saw the notification about the Queen's rare address, it said: "Washington Post – **27 mins ago**." I understand randomness, and that most believe signs are a hoax, but we create significance out of all sorts of things every day. We choose our signs, our rituals, the things that inspire us to believe. I believe that being more positive will make things so, at least in our own minds.

But about the Queen's address being posted twenty-seven minutes before. If you're going to pull off a hoax, it's nice when it seems like Oprah *and* the Queen might be in on it.

AMṚITA

DAY 25

I didn't want to pull a card like this, and certainly not on a Monday after I'd enjoyed a light-hearted Sunday, all things considered.

Amṛita means the next life, or in the next world. The immortal part of us.

Death and the afterlife are strange topics for someone raised with certain religious beliefs about heaven. When you leave a belief system behind, you'd better be an instrument-rated pilot, because you'll find yourself flying alone in the dark and defending your chosen spiritual flight path until you land. And then you'll have to defend that decision too.

I sat down to meditate, filled with apprehension. I could feel my hips not wanting to get comfortable. My neck was stiff. I tapped my fingers, closed my eyes, and dropped in. Faces were looking back at me, swirling on the inside of eyelids. They weren't as much faces as blurry features, and then they were gone.

Losing people is a mystery. Some believe our days are numbered, our hairs are counted, and there's a master plan for each of us, so when it happens, it's easier to accept. I'm not sure about that. Finding meaning in someone's death is a peculiar task for those left behind when we have no idea what truly happens to them other than what we choose to believe.

Where do they go? "To heaven," would be the Judeo-Christian response. To the next life or life cycle would be the Buddhist response. But where? Where logistically do they go? The death toll was climbing so high, and so rapidly, I stopped checking the numbers.

In 2014 I lost a cherished friend who died unexpectedly in his sleep overseas on a trip for work. Three years before that, he was the first person to whom I said the words, "I'm a writer." I don't remember why I told him of all people. We traveled together frequently for our work as board members of a large non-profit. He might have been a combination of a good listener, and someone removed far enough from my daily life with whom I felt safe sharing a secret I considered so private, so detrimental to the role I played in my professional life as a lawyer. I remember feeling the words, not just saying them. The truth will do that to you.

My friend wasn't my spouse, my sibling, my parent, or my child. So when I thought of the pain of losing someone so unexpectedly as those losing their loved ones to the virus, you can understand my discomfort trying to wrap my head around unexpected, tragic loss. The suffering was unimaginable to me. I had no point of reference for losing someone before what felt like their appropriate time other than him, my friend.

To be here with us and then gone, how is it possible? How quickly do their spirits leave? Do they get to hang around and know we miss them so awfully? Do they see how we struggle with all the love we still have for them? Where do we put it? We can't just convert it to sorrow or life lessons like exchanging money at the airport. The energy of the emotions that linger in and among us when someone disappears from our lives, it must *go* somewhere.

Three weeks after I lost my friend, after flying across the country for his wake, after the shock of it subsided, I dreamt he was in my living room. I spoke to him casually. But slowly it sunk in that he'd never been to my home, not to mention, he was dead.

When I realized I was dreaming and began to come around, I started to ask him questions in a rapid-fire barrage: "Where are you? Did you really leave? Can you come back to us? Do you visit? Are you really here?" He smiled as my wakefulness set in, and he faded away. I jumped out of bed and ran to the chair in my living room, where he sat in my dream. I wanted to believe he was really there. I wanted to think that by missing him so much, he would appear.

I've bottled the admiration I have for my friend since the day he encouraged me to write. Since his death, I've wondered what advice he might have for me since my life has taken such a turn, exacerbated by the pandemic. He was one of the most positive-thinking people I'd ever met. The only positive thing I could draw from losing him was what everyone losing a loved one was now experiencing. They will be there for us on the other side, in the amrita. We will see them again.

I intended to meditate again that evening, but I took a phone call instead. A friend was feeling scared about the changes to her employment. Three weeks before, I would have said I was channeling my dead friend's optimism and positive thinking, but as I listened to myself, it was all me. I told her it would be alright in the end, and I believed it.

VINYĀSA

DAY 26

*T*he twenty-seven-day journey was almost complete, but I was convinced it would never end. It was turning out to be just a part of the journey towards placing positive thoughts and intentions in a way that would act as stepping stones, one in front of the other. Not always smooth or even, not always round or stable, but part of the path.

Vinyāsa may be my favorite Sanskrit word. Its aesthetics are all the things our journey through life is not. Smooth, comfortable, predictable. It means: To place in a special or sacred way. The placement refers to positions of our body in yoga poses or āsanas (e.g., "down dog"), as a series of movements harmonized with the breath.

A vinyāsa's movements flow and activate different muscles, different sensations with different purposes. Often, students develop preferences for yoga instructors based on the vinyāsas he or she fashions to guide students through a class. In my experience, at the heart of every vinyāsa is the flow.

The coronavirus pandemic has played out as one of the

most flagrant examples of interrupting our flow. We didn't realize there was a flow to so many things until it was interrupted.

Several years ago, I attended a presentation given by the head of the water department in Washington, DC. The department manages thousands of miles of old pipes that deliver water to all its residents. He said the only phone calls his office ever receives are complaints because no one ever picks up the phone to say: "Hey, thanks! The water tasted great today!" He may have had the most thankless job ever.

It took a pandemic to realize we'd been treating even our most mundane routines with thanklessness. In my efforts to become a positive thinker, I noticed that gratitude was at the heart of being positive. When I meditated on the word vinyāsa, I visualized routines: Shopping at the supermarket, filling the gas tank, standing in line at the hardware store, having dinner in a restaurant. These things we took as habits or entitlements became luxurious memories in a very short period of time. It had been twenty-six days since I sat at Nirvana Grille, the last meal I enjoyed in a restaurant with a crisp bottle of wine and food that felt gorgeous on the tongue while surrounded by amazing mask-less humans in close proximity.

My commitment to practice yoga every day (even if only for twenty minutes) veered onto another course on Day Twenty-Six to be more grateful for the little things. I signed onto YogaWorks and sampled four different kinds of yoga I'd never practiced before: Iyengar, Ashtanga, Yoga Nidra, and Yin. A four-course yogic meal where I learned new ways of putting things in a special way. I wasn't successful at all of it, but I realized the value of placing my body in certain positions. Our bodies feel everything and store that information like a hard drive with an infinite capacity to remember. There is no feeling we've experienced, mental, physical, or spiritual that the body can't recall given the right prompt.

The practice of positive thinking is like a vinyāsa. It's a way to place our thoughts in a special way to train our brains not to jump to terrifying conclusions. It's about placing our thoughts outside of our mind if we must, to make room for the thoughts that will give us a reason to believe everything will be alright. Any routine we implement with ourselves to reach the place where we can push aside life's crap is as sacred as any hymn, any chant, any prayer. Even our crap is important. We just can't let it control us, to sway us away from believing we can move past it.

May you develop a vinyāsa, a way to place things in your life in a special way that gives you comfort and a belief that everything will be alright.

MANDALA

DAY 27

*O*n day twenty-seven, I invoked the scrivener's advantage: I chose the last card rather than relying on the result of a random draw. I chose the one I thought would end this journey well.

The idea of fate and acceptance was heavy on my mind. Maybe it was the sense that our country was at a stage with coronavirus where we couldn't control the illnesses and deaths, the seeds had already taken root. A certain desensitization had set in. The entire experience was still surreal enough to make it unreal to those of us who hadn't suffered the illness or known someone who had died from it.

Or maybe it was that we'd settled in for a longer haul than we expected and were doing our best to hold on to our new reality while still managing the reality we were losing.

Mandala literally means circle. But a mandala can be a physical symbol representing the universe, or a spiritual symbol of exercises, that includes meditation, where one must scale specific barriers to reach the center of the circle, to obtain the prize.

These barriers can include attaining qualities such as

purity, for example. What's in the center of the circle is the goal, and it varies according to practice, culture, and other factors. The overarching and powerful interpretation is that a mandala is a symbol of the universe, that everything is connected, and the spiritual journey is in us all.

I meditated on the concept of a circle, that no matter where you start you will go around and around with no option to break the beginning away from the end. It is an eternal connection. This was the path the virus had taken. This was the reality. We must pass through it in order to continue.

It hadn't been all bad. On Day Twenty-Three, the morose news reports were peppered with inspirational stories in between, like videos from doctors at Mt. Sinai Hospital, who had effectively split the design of available ventilators harnessing the capacity to feed oxygen from one ventilator to two patients instead of one.

On this last day, I had a deadline for a legal brief looming, the sort of writing that doesn't allow for creativity but rather requires facts and reality. The sense of the task met me on the mat for my first meditation. Where is this virus taking us factually? It's like having boarded a train and not knowing the destination. We'll be on this train until someone can make it stop, or find a treatment to live healthily until the end of the journey.

I did ten vinyasas to mimic the sense of a circle, a pattern that repeats, connects, and flows. For those who don't practice yoga, the vinyasa I did, called sun salutation "A", is a demanding pace of yoga positions that incorporates a plank, doing a push-up, half a plank, a backbend (upward facing dog), and a slight inversion (downward facing dog), and a small jump or shimmy back to standing up, all in a flowing succession, starting and stopping at the same place.

The circle is rarely ever smooth. I always have a problem

lowering from plank to the ground, my wrists and shoulders are creaky, and I'm not as strong as I used to be. It's the part of the circle of movements that causes me the most pain, the most discomfort. Most of the time, I pull through it. Sometimes I don't.

At the end of my twenty-seven-day commitment, our country was in the painful part of the vinyasa, the rough patch of the circle. We'd prepared, stretched, strengthened, and gotten ready for what was to come. The uncomfortable part, the positioning and distancing from others, the economic discomfort, the pain of loss, and the uncertainty of reaching the end. And still some of us didn't pull through.

When I meditated later in the day, I thought about the people that weren't going to make it through the rough part of this pandemic. Their bodies would fail them, or worse, the system might fail them.

A mandala is a symbol of endurance, discipline, and harmony. It can take us from comfortable to painful. This COVID-19 mandala is a brutal circle of stamina, and those who survive but watch others pass will find themselves in their own mandalas, fighting through the devastation and seeking the comfort and recovery from the loss of loved ones. Everyone will have a story.

My journey has been an exercise in practicing the positiveness we can bring into our lives and those around us when we endeavor not to become our emotions.You are not yours; I am not mine. It has been my mandala, my guiding principle.

I'd tried so hard during the beginning of this journey to be a source of positiveness. I even tried to smile as much as I could when looking at other people. I once told a grocery store worker that I was smiling at them when I knew they couldn't see my mouth behind my mask. I smiled and looked at people even in traffic, knowing they were doing the best they could, as was I. Humans are built to rise and fall, to live through the highest of highs and the lowest of lows.

I completed the final meditation for this book with the intention of sending hope for those whose lives were taken, and those they left behind. I smiled so big during my meditation that my eyes watered from squinting. There is nothing we can do when the mandala of this part of our lives doesn't include those we've lost. There's no way to move forward towards the next blind turn on the circle without merely a desire for better, and gratitude for what and who we still have.

My final meditation felt like the beginning and not the end of something. Something that would be better for us all in the end, no matter how bad the changes in our lives felt. Transformation isn't comfortable, but being positive and open to the change will bring great rewards. That's how I chose to look at it.

And so, the sun set on Day Twenty-Seven.

EPILOGUE

*P*ositive thinking didn't magically inhabit me after this twenty-seven-day practice, just like having children doesn't suddenly make you a patient person.

Nor was positive thinking a solution I found to fix all my problems. But when I committed to it, my problems seemed more like a process to navigate through toward the next phase of life rather than roadblocks full of panic and dread. When I started to think of it that way, the next phase of life, although a complete mystery, didn't paralyze me with fear.

Positive thinking gave me a set of tools to feel more curious about the the future. At the end of the twenty-seven days, I felt less "why is this happening to me?" and more, "wow, I wonder where this is leading me?"

I can report that on the day I published, I was still grateful, and still thinking positively. Not because it had gotten easier, but because it became a habit I stuck with to derail the doomy, gloomy gremlins that slink around the hallways of my mind. The struggle is real, but so are the results.

ACKNOWLEDGMENTS

After completing my twenty-seven-day commitment to positive thinking via practicing yoga, meditation, and randomly selected Sanskrit words, I decided it was time to become more educated as to all three.

I enrolled in a 200-hour yoga teacher training course via YogaWorks which allowed for an online teaching experience. To say this was an ambitious undertaking during a pandemic is an understatement. Yet, it was one of the most fulfilling experiences of my life. The course didn't make me an expert, just the opposite. It was the sort of education that made me realize how much I don't know. And that is utterly and magically exciting.

I want to acknowledge every one of my classmates in that rigorous six week training session; an international community of twenty-seven (yes, twenty-seven) amazing souls who chose to show up during the pandemic and commit to a life change. From the United States, to England, to Germany, to Greece, to India, to Sri Lanka. You, my amazing yoga compatriots, know who you are. What a blessing to know that between all of our different time zones, one of you is always awake and shining your light in the world no matter what time I look at the clock. Thank you for holding space for me. We are eternally connected.

Also, I want to send love, light, praise, humor, and gorgeous thoughts to our teacher trainers Anna Zorzou, Ashley Rideaux, Jennie Cohen, and Jeanne Heileman who led us through the most amazing and "juicy" physical, mental, and spiritual experiences that could have ever occurred during a pandemic. And of course, the models of yogic instruction, Penelopi and Theo. And a special thank you to my weekly pre-pandemic YogaWorks guides, Renee Chenette and L.B. Iddings. You both held torches lighting the way down my yogic path, whether you knew it or not.

I honor all of your beautiful spirits housed inside those beautiful bodies with those beautiful minds and hearts.

Namaste.

BIBLIOGRAPHY

$\mathcal{W}$ ith gratitude, the following resources were available at my fingertips:

KRANS, Kim. The Wild Unknown Animal Spirit Deck & Guidebook. New York, NY. HarperOne, 2018.

IYENGAR, B.K.S. *Light on Yoga*. New York: Schocken, 1979.

LOWITZ, Leeza, and Datta, Reema. *Sacred Sanskrit Words For Yoga, Chant, and Meditation*. Berkeley, California. Stone Bridge Press. 2005.

SATCHIDANANDA SS. *The Yoga Sutras of Patanjali*. Buckingham, Virginia: Integral Yoga Publications; *2012.*

· · ·

With more gratitude, these resources were available online:

www.americansanskrit.com

Website of the American Sanskrit Institute, created by Vyaas Houston.

www.ananda.org

The official website for the Ananda Church of Self-Realization of Nevada County which teaches "effective techniques for expanding a sense of self, such as meditation, Kriya Yoga, spiritual Hatha Yoga, and divine friendship."

www.ancient.eu

A non-profit company publishing a history encyclopedia. Their mission is to engage people with cultural heritage and to improve history education worldwide.

www.britannica.com

The website of Britannica Group, Inc. offers empowerment in the world teaches and learns.

www.cdc.gov

The Centers for Disease Control and Prevention website with daily updates of corona virus 2019 (COVID-19) cases and deaths.

www.eastern-spirituality.com

A great reference for definitions of Vedic/Hindu & Buddhist spiritual terms.

www.esalen.org
The website for the Esalen center founded in 1962 by Michael Murphy and Dick Price, located in Big Sur, California.

WWW.HQ.NASA.GOV/ALSJ/A11/A11.LANDING.HTML
NASA website with transcripts and audio recordings of various NASA missions, including the first lunar landing July 20, 1969.

WWW.NEWWORLDENCYCLOPEDIA.ORG
The website for the New World Encyclopedia project.

www.sanskrit.org
The website of the Sanskrit Religious Institute, offering chants and information about the Hindu religion and traditions.
www.smithsonianmag.com
The website of the Smithsonian Magazine.

www.spokensanskrit.org
An online hypertext dictionary of Sanskrit definitions.

www.theguardian.com

Reader-funded news source covering American and international news for an online global audience.

THETHIRTY.WHOWHATWEAR.COM/HOW-TO-SET-INTENTIONS
Sister-site of Who What Wear.

www.verywellmind.com
Online resources for mental health resources.

www.yogajournal.com
The website of the print magazine Yoga Journal.

www.yogapedia.com
An online yoga encyclopedia.

www.yogateket.com
An online yoga community offering online yoga classes and resources.

ABOUT THE AUTHOR

AND EDITOR

Sola Damon is the pseudonym for a survivor of a twenty-year legal career as a trial lawyer. Born in the United States, she lived out her childhood in the West Indies and South Florida where she maintains strong ties. Sola writes fiction and small memoirs about slices of life. She adores the written word, her two stepsons, and daughter-in-law. She resides in Fort Lauderdale, Florida, and Laguna Beach, California and maintains a strong presence with extended family in the West Indies.

www.soladamon.com

ABOUT THE EDITOR

Susan VandeLinde is a proof-editor with a flair for the earthy and serene. She lends her skills to make writers look amazing, not only in print but in fashion. She is the creator of Damselfly Jewelry, where she designs elegant and urban creations to frost her clients with pure, elegant beauty.